classroom
LIFE
SAVERS

PETER
CLUTTERBUCK

Level Three

Ashton Scholastic

SYDNEY AUCKLAND NEW YORK TORONTO LONDON

To the memory of Martin Carboon

The purchase of this book entitles the teacher to reproduce the black-line masters for classroom use.

Copyright © Peter Clutterbuck, 1987

First published in 1987 by Ashton Scholastic Pty Limited (Inc in NSW)
PO Box 579 Gosford NSW 2250

Also in Brisbane, Melbourne, Adelaide, Perth and Auckland NZ

Typeset by Gardiner Initiates Pty Limited, Gosford, NSW
Printed by Star Printery Pty Limited, Erskinville, NSW

10 9 8 7 6 5 4   0 1 2 3 / 9

classroom
LIFE
SAVERS

Introduction

How many times during the school day do you wish there was something extra to give the class? Students often finish work early, have free time, need inspiring on rainy days, want a refreshing change to the usual homework tasks or need a 'brain warmer' at certain times of the day. CLASSROOM LIFESAVERS rescues you from all those moments.

For students who are coping more than adequately with a particular area of the curriculum there is nothing to be gained in providing more of the same. Such practices create a great deal of boredom and frustration for the learner.

The problem of catering for students who consistently finish their work earlier than the rest of the class has long concerned teachers. The class teacher is so often occupied with assisting the slower learners that little effort can be make in providing worthwhile activities for these children.

CLASSROOM LIFESAVERS has been designed to provide the challenges these children so desperately need. Activities are carefully graded in six major areas.

1   Language
2   Mathematics
3   General Knowledge and Vocabulary
4   Teasers and Logical Puzzles
5   Observation and Memory
6   Games for Two or Three

There is no preparation needed by the class teacher as the activities are self-explanatory and apart from a pencil and paper generally no other equipment is needed.

A reproducible Student Record is included and answers are provided at the back of the book.

With the exception of the Observation and Memory section, activities have been designed so that they can be photocopied and mounted on cards. The cards can then be kept in a box in an easily accessible area. Early finishers may then go and get a card and continue quietly without disturbing the rest of the class.

There are, however, no hard and fast rules – in fact the activities will lend themselves to a multitude of uses. Substitute teachers will wonder how they ever survived without LIFESAVERS – a wealth of fully reproducible activity sheets ready to use with students of any level.

Level Three is designed for use with students in Years 5-7. Level One provides individual, fully-reproducible worksheets for Years 1-3 and Level Two caters for Years 3-5 in a similar format to Level Three.

However you use them, CLASSROOM LIFESAVERS will make every minute in the classroom count. They will spark every student's idle moment.

Student Record

Name:

Word Puzzles	1	2	3	4	5	6	7	8	9	10	11	12	13	14	15	16	17	18	19	20
	21	22	23	24	25	26	27	28	29	30	31	32	33	34	35	36	37	38	39	40
Maths Puzzles	1	2	3	4	5	6	7	8	9	10	11	12	13	14	15	16	17	18	19	20
Observation and Memory	1	2	3	4	5	6	7	8	9	10	11	12	13	14	15	16	17	18	19	20
General Knowledge and Vocabulary	1	2	3	4	5	6	7	8	9	10	11	12	13	14	15	16	17	18	19	20
Teasers and Logical Puzzles	1	2	3	4	5	6	7	8	9	10	11	12	13	14	15	16	17	18	19	20
Games for 2 or 3	1	2	3	4	5	6	7	8	9	10										

Word-puzzles

Left-out letters

A   In the following you are given the last four letters of ten
six-letter words. Write the word. (There may be more than one answer.)

1 — — ncil   4 — — nnis   7 — — cape
2 — — llow   5 — — cket   8 — — ange
3 — — ison   6 — — anet   9 — — gine

B   Add two letters to make the six-letter word which fits the definition.

1 — — nkey – stubborn animal   7 — — rple – colour
2 — — edle – pointed sewing tool 8 — — upid – silly
3 — — lver – metal   9 — — hlia – flower
4 — — onde – fair   10 — — ttle – livestock
5 — — bbit – small, furry animal 11 — — llad – song
6 — — ntre – middle   12 — — nnel – hole

Word-puzzles

Anagrams

A   Anagrams are words made by rearranging the letters of a given
word eg blow = bowl. You must use all the letters in the new
word. Make another word by rearranging these letters.

1 bleat   4 low   7 earth
2 peach   5 war   8 fringe
3 charm   6 flow   9 shore

B   This time, rearrange the letters of each word twice to make two new words.

1 amen   4 edit   7 lame
2 tame   5 slime   8 sprite
3 dare   6 lair   9 acre

Making words

A Make as many words as you can by using the letters in the grid. Each word must contain the large letter and the other letters may only be used once.

E		
m	a	
t	s	
d	h	
p	d	r	c

B How many names of animals can you make from the grid below? To spell an animal, keep moving from one letter to another in any direction – up, down, across, diagonally. You may move in several different directions for each word. 'Mouse' has been done for you.

C	H	T	P	L
O	A	D	I	O
E	R	O	G	N
B	S	E	O	M
T	A	U	L	U

Word pieces

A The paper on which we had the following words written has been torn in half. Can you help by joining the word on the left with a word on the right to make a new word?

1 no			pear
2 short			tack
3 host			age
4 ram			ridge
5 at			hand
6 reap			let
7 pat			mad
8 cart			page
9 brace			tern

B Take one letter from the the first word and place it somewhere in the second word to make two words with the same meanings.

eg chew how = hew chop

1 skill laughter ⎯⎯⎯⎯⎯⎯⎯

2 pier tat ⎯⎯⎯⎯⎯⎯⎯

3 ripe tar ⎯⎯⎯⎯⎯⎯⎯

4 lone singe ⎯⎯⎯⎯⎯⎯⎯

5 shred ban ⎯⎯⎯⎯⎯⎯⎯

6 boast hip ⎯⎯⎯⎯⎯⎯⎯

7 cult sash ⎯⎯⎯⎯⎯⎯⎯

8 blare bad ⎯⎯⎯⎯⎯⎯⎯

Word-puzzles

Missing letters

A The following words have 'e' or 'ee' missing. Write the word putting in the missing letters.

1 plas ———	5 lvn ———	9 coff ———
2 flc ———	6 agl ———	10 jwl ———
3 stl ———	7 vry ———	11 chs ———
4 tr ———	8 grn ———	12 fnc ———

B In the following words 'i' has been left out. Write the word putting in the missing letters.

1 shrt ———	5 knfe ———	9 sprt ———
2 flm ———	6 shp ———	10 slver ———
3 fnsh ———	7 drty ———	11 sad ———
4 skppng ———	8 drecton ———	12 polce ———

Word puzzles

Jumbled words

A Unjumble the letters to make a word.

1 mdru	6 huts
2 estb	7 elph
3 opeh	8 rawd
4 artc	9 aldo
5 hint	10 guyl

Missing vowels

B The vowels have been left out of the names of the names of these birds. Enter the vowels to find the bird.

1 k—k—b—rr	6 v—lt—r
2 k—w—	7 b—dg—r—g—r
3 sp—rr—w	8 p— —c—ck
4 p—rr—t	9 p—l—c—n
5 fl—m—ng	10 thr—sh

Word puzzles

Word pieces

A   Make two five-letter words in each row by joining the letter groups together,
eg out sh rt ski = shout skirt

1 ife   kn   one   al —————————
2 sn   ble   ta   ake —————————
3 uld   mo   wo   ney —————————
4 rst   bu   ast   co —————————
5 mu   ush   br   sic —————————

6 ag   rty   di   ain —————————
7 zen   cl   do   iff —————————
8 air   ma   ch   tch —————————
9 ast   to   ize   pr —————————
10 ery   qu   ev   ick —————————

B   Make two six-letter words in each row by joining the letter groups together.

1 aid   nic   pic   afr —————————
2 and   isl   fel   low —————————
3 ple   ani   pur   mal —————————
4 son   sea   fol   low —————————
5 lve   ing   dur   twe —————————

6 ven   cor   hea   ner —————————
7 ine   eng   row   nar —————————
8 nat   sil   ure   ver —————————
9 eum   mus   pig   eon —————————
10 bri   dle   bun   dge —————————

Word puzzles

'Cat' words

A   Each of these words begins with 'cat'. A clue has been given to help you.

1 This cat is a sailing boat.
2 This cat is a large church.
3 This cat is found at Sunday school.
4 This cat is a calamity.
5 This cat is a book of things for sale.
6 This cat is used for shooting.
7 This cat is on a farm.
8 This cat is a grub.
9 This cat is a waterfall.
10 This cat is a brief sleep.

'Car' words

B   Each of these words begins with 'car'.

1 A car that is a large moose.
2 A car that eats flesh.
3 A car on television.
4 A car which is a mobile home.
5 A car in a gun shop.
6 A car you wear.
7 A car in a flower garden.
8 A car in a vegetable garden.
9 A car on the floor.
10 A car used for wine.

Word puzzles

Hidden words

A Take letters from the end of the first word and beginning of the second word to make names of metals or precious stones.

eg zebras scatter = brass

1 gale advances ――――――――

2 snick elephant ――――――――

3 shrub yellow ――――――――

4 stir once ――――――――

5 hop always ――――――――

6 vast increase ――――――――

7 biggest eels ――――――――

8 going olden ――――――――

9 fossil verse ――――――――

10 quiz include ――――――――

B Take letters from the end of the first word and from the beginning of the second word to make the names of insects.

eg Herman tanks = ant

1 show aspirations ――――――――

2 sign attack ――――――――

3 graph idioms ――――――――

4 abhor nettles ――――――――

5 hello user ――――――――

6 ewe evils ――――――――

7 hello customer ――――――――

8 clear wiggle ――――――――

9 brief leave ――――――――

10 eskimo throw ――――――――

Word puzzles

Hidden birds

A The following small words complete the names of birds. What is each bird?

1 ―――――― over

2 ―――――― ant

3 ―――――― rich

4 ―――――― ken

5 ―――――― low

6 ―――――― rush

7 ―――――― row

8 ―――――― can

9 ―――――― pie

B The name of a bird is hidden in each of these sentences. Can you find it?

eg We have a micro wave – crow

1 I saw the pigs wallowing in the mud.

2 After the race he began to puff in great huffs.

3 I watched the bright star linger in the sky.

4 Michael has a painful throb in his arm.

5 This nib is broken.

6 The sea gleams in the sunshine.

7 The cupboard is high, awkward and too large.

8 I saw her on the swing.

Back-to-front words

A   The first part of each word has been written last. What is each word?

eg orrowtom = tomorrow

1 bandhus _____

2 fulbeauti _____

3 ingwrit _____

4 latechoco _____

5 toestoma _____

6 ctricele _____

7 bonrib _____

8 tablevege _____

9 oonball _____

10 waysal _____

Stars and stripes

B   Americans have developed different words to us for many common everyday things. Match the word we use in Australia with its American counterpart.

Australian word	American word
scone	candy
petrol	street-car
holiday	muffin
lollies	gasoline
luggage	automobile
timetable	vacation
footpath	soda-pop
soft drink	baggage
car	sidewalk
tram	schedule

Dropping letters

A   Drop one letter from the word on the left to make a word that fits the definition.

1 store – ripped up

2 flour – a number

3 cheap – a man

4 leather – soapy

5 chair – covering of the head

6 steal – an animal

7 calves – holes in the earth

8 heart – warmth

9 spare – to fight

10 home – a digging tool

Adding letters

B   Add a letter to the end of the word on the left to make a word that fits the definition.

eg den – mark made by a blow = dent

1 tall – total

2 modes – unassuming

3 gull – narrow valley

4 came – an animal

5 stamped – fleeing animals

6 came – a carved gem

7 year – desire deeply

8 sting – mean, miserly

9 grim – dirt

10 heart – fireside

Word puzzles

Missing letters

A You are given the middle three letters of ten five-letter words. You must add one letter at the front and one at the end to make the word. (Answers may differ in some cases.)
eg __uni__ =tunic

1 __lov__
2 __ote__
3 __air__
4 __irt__
5 __ort__

6 __nai__
7 __ruc__
8 __eav__
9 __elo__
10 __orc__

Hidden words

B If you cross out every second letter you will find the name of a living creature.

1 pvoprbpdoxicsnet
2 pbloavtdynpmuzsx
3 pmyptzhxoynv
4 lxiyzpatrody
5 rpebianxdtepeyri

6 hbacmbsttgehri
7 paibrcadnehfag
8 pmenloipcqarns
9 felfagmhijnkglom
10 bpumftfvanlyoz

Word puzzles

Animal mysteries

A The vowels have been left out of the names of these animals. Can you put them back to discover the name of each animal?

1 ch___t_h
2 __l__ph__nt
3 b__ff__l__
4 b__b___n
5 g__r__ll__

6 h__dg__h__g
7 g__r__ff__
8 f__rr__t
9 m__ng___s__
10 sq__rr__l

One word for many

B One word in each line is a name for all the others together. Find that word.
eg autumn (season) winter spring

1 sycamore   ash   oak   tree
2 hammer   tool   screwdriver   chisel
3 mutton   venison   beef   meat
4 sparrow   thrush   bird   starling
5 fruit   apple   plum   peach
6 crimson   azure   colour   khaki
7 furniture   chair   lounge   table
8 copper   metal   iron   gold
9 vegetable   carrot   turnip   cabbage
10 plaice   fish   herring   mackerel

Word puzzles

Puzzling words

A   Each of these puzzles contains a familiar word or phrase. Can you write what each one says.
eg lofallve = fall <u>in</u> love

1 s_t
    a
     r
      s

        fed
4 I'm

2 F_lO_oR_sE_tS T

3 <u>long</u>
   due

         look
5 look   you   look
         look

B Now make up your own for these:

1 knock before you enter
2 don't look up
3 broken heart
4 one in a million

Word puzzles

Fruits

Hidden in this word grid are fifteen fruits. Can you find them and write them on a sheet of paper? Words are written up, down, across and backwards.

L	E	M	O	N	H	T	A	Q
A	P	P	L	E	C	O	N	U
P	E	L	I	M	A	M	A	I
R	A	U	V	I	E	A	N	N
I	R	M	E	L	P	T	A	C
C	H	E	R	R	Y	O	B	E
O	R	A	N	G	E	N	T	T
T	G	I	F	M	A	N	G	O

Word puzzles

Parts of the body

Hidden in this word grid are twenty parts of the body. Can you find them and write them on a sheet of paper? Words are written up, down, across and backwards.

Z	S	N	G	T	X	W	V	T
S	K	E	L	E	T	O	N	O
M	U	C	A	E	S	B	I	E
R	L	K	N	T	I	L	K	S
A	L	N	D	H	R	E	S	E
E	Y	E	S	X	W	A	J	U
T	M	E	N	R	I	B	S	G
Z	P	X	L	I	V	E	R	N
V	T	B	E	A	R	D	V	O
M	O	U	T	H	E	A	R	T

Word puzzles

Colours

Hidden in this word grid are fourteen colours. Can you find them and write them on a sheet of paper? Words are written up, down, across and backwards.

G	R	E	E	N	Y	E	W
O	R	A	N	G	E	L	H
L	E	Z	Z	R	L	P	I
D	D	B	T	E	L	R	T
E	U	L	B	Y	O	U	E
T	X	A	Z	Z	W	P	N
A	V	C	R	E	A	M	W
N	Z	K	N	I	P	T	A
B	R	O	W	N	Z	Z	F

Word puzzles

Clothing

Hidden in this word grid are twenty pieces of clothing. Can you find them and write them on a sheet of paper? Words are written up, down, across and backwards.

P	Y	J	A	M	A	S	T	S
T	V	L	P	T	A	H	S	M
S	C	A	R	F	T	I	E	O
K	O	D	O	R	L	R	V	C
I	A	N	N	O	E	T	O	K
R	T	A	V	C	B	W	L	K
T	X	S	E	K	W	T	G	C
D	R	E	S	S	U	I	T	O
C	A	P	T	E	R	E	B	S
T	R	O	U	S	E	R	S	W

Word puzzles

Inside the home

Hidden in this word grid are sixteen common things found in the home. Can you find them and write them on a sheet of paper? Words are written up, down, across and backwards.

X	C	A	R	P	E	T	X	T
C	U	P	B	O	A	R	D	R
F	R	Y	P	A	N	A	N	E
S	T	O	V	E	G	D	E	C
L	A	M	P	T	U	I	V	U
M	I	R	R	O	R	O	O	A
K	N	I	F	E	A	F	O	S
S	P	O	O	N	I	S	A	B
T	E	L	E	P	H	O	N	E

Word puzzles

Left-out letters

A   Here are the last four letters of ten seven-letter words. Use the clues to help you decide what each word is.

1 _____laud   clap
2 _____take   error
3 _____lage   town
4 _____iday   vacation
5 _____tion   train stop

6 _____unia   flower
7 _____mate   weather
8 _____ssom   flower
9 _____ress   home
10 _____nket   bed covering

B   In the following words the middle five letters are given. Put two letters in front and two letters behind to make the word that fits the clue.

1 _____nderf_____   terrific
2 _____ocola_____   sweet
3 _____thedr_____   large church
4 _____auffe_____   drives a car
5 _____batro_____   seabird

6 _____rmala_____   a jam
7 _____lepho_____   used for messages
8 _____haust_____   very tired
9 _____lario_____   very funny
10 _____nnequ_____   model

Word puzzles

Anagrams

A   Make the number of words in the brackets by using all the letters of the given word.

1 deigns (3)
2 enlist (4)
3 tops (4)
4 solemn (2)
5 least (4)

6 aster (3)
7 seaside (1)
8 mesa (2)
9 swine (2)
10 battle (1)

Add-a-word anagram

B   Add a letter to the given word, rearrange the letters and make a new word that matches the clue in the brackets.

eg heap (a fruit) = peach

1 ache (near the ocean)
2 brute (a servant)
3 this (a garment)
4 care (to frighten)
5 dear (a food)
6 seat (a large meal)
7 retain (sure)
8 lines (quiet)

Making words

A How many words can you make from the letters in the grid? Use each of the other letters only once. Each word must contain the central letters. No plurals are allowed.

G	I	N
E	L	M
Y	E	S

Fruit salad

B Use the words in the list to complete the Fruit Salad word puzzle. Each word will fit in only one position.

F _ _   guava
_ _ _ R _ _   apricot
_ U _ _ _   raisin
_ I _ _   fig
_ _ _ _ _ _ _ T   pear

_ _ _ S _ _   cherry
_ _ A _   mango
_ L _ _   avocado
_ A _ _ _   lime
_ _ _ _ _ D _   plum

Word pieces

A Add one word from the first column, one word in the second column and one word in the third column to make a new word.

1 sat   ice   factory
2 at   ten   cent
3 lieu tend ate
4 can   is   ant
5 for   no   ten
6 in   get   ant
7 to   did   able
8 not   got   her

_____
_____
_____
_____
_____
_____
_____
_____

B Move a letter from one word into the other word making two words with the same meaning.
eg hop chew = chop hew

1 slave   savage
2 tore   smart
3 spiny   grate
4 bawl   fright
5 shovel hack
6 farce   font
7 sore   stave
8 march   doe

_____ _____
_____ _____
_____ _____
_____ _____
_____ _____
_____ _____
_____ _____
_____ _____

Word puzzles

Missing letters

A In the following words the letter 'o' is missing. Add the letter 'o' where necessary to complete each word.

1 fld _____
2 chclate _____
3 crd _____
4 vice _____
5 cttn _____

6 sup _____
7 blssm _____
8 chse _____
9 famus _____
10 cugh _____

B In the following words the letter 'b' is missing. Add the letter 'b' where necessary to complete the word.

1 caage _____
2 alloon _____
3 prolem _____
4 reak _____
5 lirary _____

6 proaly _____
7 ule _____
8 doule _____
9 moile _____
10 golet _____

Word puzzles

Jumbled words

A Unjumble the letters to make each word.

| 1 ritge | 3 whtro | 5 tahbi | 7 slgas | 9 dofun |
| 2 yspan | 4 yohne | 6 aezbr | 8 lacme | 10 tigan |

Missing consonants

B Here are the names of popular sports or pastimes but their consonants are missing. Put in the missing consonants and complete each word. (Each __ represents one letter.)

1 _ o _ _
2 _ e _ _ i _
3 _ _ i _ _ e _
4 _ _ i i _ _
5 _ o _ e _

6 _ o _ _ _ a _ _
7 _ o _ _ i _ _
8 _ _ e _ _
9 _ o _ i _ _
10 a _ _ _ e _ i _ _

Word make

A Join pairs of letters from each group to make two six-letter words.
eg ju ho ng ll le ow = jungle hollow

1 bu st ab le ck et
2 sh la sp et ck ti
3 mo me ch nt ur ch
4 ca po tt ck le et
5 ch sh ee ou se ld
6 su br mm an er ch
7 er lv si le ab st
8 tt bu on po li ce

B Make two nine-letter words from each row by linking the groups of letters.

1 ams eym hon oon ogr kil
2 orc hes tra scu ure lpt
3 col orc lec tra hes tor
4 ima sec ary gin ret ary
5 ure scu han age lpt orp
6 ery eme dis rge cov ncy
7 ate nas gym hib ium ern
8 cas eta ser ble ole veg

'Ant' words

A Find the word that contains 'ant'. Use the clues to help you.

1 _____ant   a large animal with trunk
2 ant_____   a piece of music
3 ant_____   very old
4 ant_____   a collection of poems
5 ant_____   a deer's horn

'Art' words

B Find the word that contains 'art'. Use the clues to help you.

1 _____art   to begin
2 _____art   navigator's map
3 _____art   organ of the body
4 art_____   an imitation, not natural
5 art_____   a tube that carries blood through the body

Word puzzles

Hidden words

A Join the letters from the end of the first word to letters at the beginning of the second word and make the names of fruits.

eg lame lonely = melon

1 urban analysers _____
2 bottle monkeys _____
3 orator angers _____
4 strap pleases _____
5 German gophers _____

6 custom atomic _____
7 lolly cheese _____
8 stirrup earliest _____
9 mannequin celebrates _____
10 tape aches _____

B Join the letters from the end of the first word to letters at the beginning of the second word and make the names of foods.

eg leave always = veal

1 babe effective _____
2 sombre advances _____
3 camel ambles _____
4 aeroplanes altitude _____
5 isthmus tardiness _____

6 rebut termites _____
7 haste welder _____
8 acre ambles _____
9 sincere always _____
10 strip early _____

Word puzzles

Hidden animals

A The following small words form the ends of the names of animals. What is each animal?

1 _____bat
2 _____ant
3 _____ale
4 _____son
5 _____by

6 _____at
7 _____bit
8 _____key
9 _____pine
10 _____sum

B In each of these sentences an animal is hidden. Can you find it?

eg Please go at once! – goat

1 I saw him grab bits of bread from the table.
2 Tim came long after the others had gone.
3 Michael hopes to be a very good boy today.
4 Don't let the boys wander away.
5 I watched the girls nail up the sign.

A Hidden females

Find the name of the female animal which is hidden in the word printed next to the name of the male.

1 boar	sowing
2 buck	does
3 ram	sewer
4 bull	scowl
5 gander	gooseberry

B Changing words

Change the first letter of each word to make a word that fits the definition.

eg hinder – a particle left in a fire = cinder

1 hamper – spoil with kindness _____

2 medication – devotion _____

3 bloat – enjoy the defeat of others _____

4 drawl – a fight _____

5 bubble – broken pieces of stone _____

A Time for a change

Change the first letter of each word to make a word that fits the clue.

eg hinder – a particle left in a fire = cinder

1 village – to loot, plunder _____

2 burrow – trench _____

3 wilt – Scottish dress _____

4 curable – lasting _____

5 raffle – to puzzle _____

B Getting ahead

Add a letter to the beginning of each word to make a word that fits the clue.

eg log – block up =clog

1 warm	crowd around	_____
2 tow	put away	_____
3 heath	a case for a sword	_____
4 bony	hard, black wood	_____
5 listen	shiny	_____

A Centre pieces

Add one letter to the start of each word and one at the end to make a word.
(Clue: all the words begin with the same letter.)

1 __aren__   3 __enci__   5 __alac__   7 __eopl__   9 __icni__
2 __ickl__   4 __arad__   6 __astr__   8 __arro__   10 __oetr__

B Two-in-one crossout

In each of the following groups of letters two words are hidden. Combine every second letter to make each word. Use the clues to help you.

1 c m r a i g c p k i e e t   _____ _____
Find a bird and a sport

2 h b o e r a n g e l t e   _____ _____
Find an insect and a dog

3 h s e u r g m a i r t   _____ _____
Find a man who lives alone and something sweet

4 p p y y r j a a m m i a d s   _____ _____
Find a large, ancient tomb and nightware

A Tricky vowels

In each word a vowel has been left out. Can you add the correct vowel to complete the word?

eg defin__te = definite

1 num__rous   6 spect__cle
2 fatig__e   7 emph__sis
3 re__lise   8 prod__gy
4 schol__r   9 fel__ny
5 hygi__ne   10 cust__dy

B Out-of-place words

One word in each line is out of place. Can you find each one?

1 corgi, spaniel, collie, chihuahua, siamese
2 car, bus, taxi, lorry, plough
3 golf, chess, rugby, cricket, football
4 painter, typist, optician, optimist, chauffeur
5 table, settee, window, stool, bookcase
6 corporal, sergeant, lieutenant, sailor, colonel
7 daffodil, rose, jonquil, carnation, apricot
8 serial, cereal, wheat, oats, barley

Drop a letter

A   **(i)** By dropping one letter at a time, change the word STARTLING into eight familiar words. Once you take a letter out you cannot put it back.

(ii) The word THEREIN contains ten words without rearranging any of the letters. What are these ten words?

Special words

B   Each of the words below is unusual for some reason. Can you discover what makes them so unusual?

1 facetious
2 indivisibility
3 hijinks

4 queue
5 subbookkeeper
6 strength

Colours

Study the word grid carefully and write down all the colours you can find. You should be able to find sixteen.

R	U	S	T	M	A	R	O	O	N
E	M	E	R	A	L	D	T	T	L
P	A	P	M	G	K	H	A	K	I
P	U	I	C	E	R	I	S	E	M
O	V	A	A	N	T	R	O	S	E
C	E	M	L	T	B	E	I	G	E
V	X	B	I	A	U	B	U	R	N
W	T	E	L	S	I	E	N	N	A
T	U	R	Q	U	O	I	S	E	V

Animals

There are twenty animals hidden in the grid. Their names are written across, down, backwards or diagonally. Find each one and write its name on a sheet of paper.

G	I	R	A	F	F	E	B	E
O	T	T	E	R	M	M	A	S
R	A	B	B	I	T	I	B	U
I	D	E	E	I	M	N	O	O
L	E	A	A	V	S	X	O	M
L	E	R	V	L	I	O	N	K
A	R	S	E	L	K	F	N	N
M	F	E	R	R	E	T	A	U
U	C	A	M	E	L	O	P	K
P	O	L	E	C	A	T	E	S

Sports

Find all the fifteen sports in the grid. Words may be forwards, backwards, horizontal, vertically or diagonally. Find each one and write its name on a piece of paper.

A	T	H	L	E	T	I	C	S	V
R	U	G	B	Y	T	M	O	K	F
C	R	I	C	K	E	T	S	I	L
H	O	C	K	E	Y	V	A	I	O
E	W	M	T	D	I	V	I	N	G
R	I	J	U	D	O	Y	L	G	O
Y	N	V	T	E	N	N	I	S	L
T	G	N	I	X	O	B	N	P	O
M	H	H	I	K	I	N	G	Z	P

Birds

There are twenty birds hidden in this grid. Can you find them all? Write each one on a piece of paper.

E	A	G	L	E	N	E	R	W
M	L	A	R	K	I	W	I	O
U	B	U	Z	Z	A	R	D	O
W	A	G	T	A	I	L	U	D
E	T	H	R	U	S	H	C	P
L	R	A	V	E	N	O	K	E
R	O	B	I	N	V	W	W	C
U	S	I	B	I	S	L	A	K
C	S	W	A	N	Z	M	H	E
C	R	O	W	D	O	V	E	R

Occupations

There are sixteen occupations hidden in the grid. Can you find them all and write them on a sheet of paper.

A	R	C	H	I	T	E	C	T
P	U	B	L	I	S	H	E	R
I	S	U	R	G	E	O	N	A
A	H	T	S	I	P	Y	T	N
R	E	H	C	T	U	B	T	S
I	A	C	T	O	R	H	C	L
S	R	A	N	G	E	R	H	A
T	E	R	E	H	C	A	E	T
Z	R	T	O	L	I	P	F	O
Y	P	P	L	U	M	B	E	R
J	O	C	K	E	Y	T	M	Y
X	R	O	Y	E	V	R	U	S

Maths puzzles

1. What are four consecutive numbers under 10 that add up to 22?

2. You are given three numbers, an equals sign and a total. Keeping the order of the numbers the same and using +, −, or × make the three numbers equal the total.

   a) 3   3   10 = 19   c) 7   7   6 = 0
   b) 9   3   6 = 2   d) 8   3   5 = 1

3. How many zeros do you use when you write ten thousand?

4. You are the sixth person in a queue and there are seven people behind the person in front of you. How many people are there in the queue?

5. What do these numbers have common?

   13 9 7 23

Maths puzzles

1. Tommy has three times as many blue socks as purple socks. There are twelve pairs altogether. How many blue socks has he?

2. Michael lives in a house that is fifth from one end of the row of houses and sixth from the other end. How many houses in the row?

3. Add all the digits from 1 to 9.

4. If you divide this number by four the answer is twice the amount you divided by. What is the number?

5. Gaylene bought six dozen dozen eggs. Wendy bought half-a-dozen dozen. Who bought the most eggs and how many more were there?

Maths puzzles

1   Here are nine squares arranged in rows of three. Arrange the digits 1 to 9 in the squares so that no matter in which direction you add – across, down or diagonally they will always total 15.

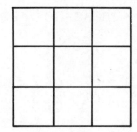

2   Put a digit inside each circle so that each side of the triangle adds up to 17. Use each of the numbers from 1 to 6

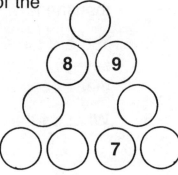

Maths puzzles

1   Look carefully at the diagram below. How many rectangles can you see?

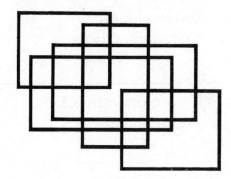

2   The dots below are joined by four straight lines. Draw the dots on a sheet of paper and join them using three straight lines.

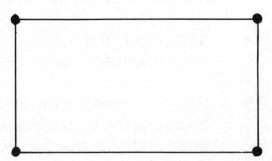

Maths puzzles

1   Arrange six coins like this. Rearrange the pattern so that each arm has four coins.

2   Copy the dot pattern onto a sheet of paper. Now rule one straight line through enough dots to leave only four dots in each row across and down.

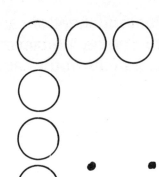

Maths puzzles

1   Arrange three coins like this, ie the middle one tails-up and the other two heads-up. Make three moves, turning over two coins each time, to finish with all three coins tails-up.

2   A young girl has three canaries which she keeps in separate cages. Yesterday her uncle gave her another canary so now she has four, however she does not have enough money to buy another cage. Can you make four cages all the same size by moving around the three she has now? Use matches to help you work it out.

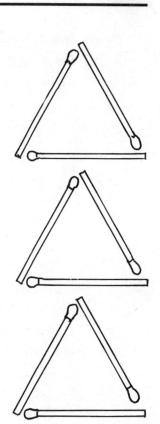

Maths puzzles

Copy the shape below onto a sheet of cardboard and cut it into the pieces shown. Shuffle the pieces and have someone time how long it takes you to arrange them into the original 'T' shape.

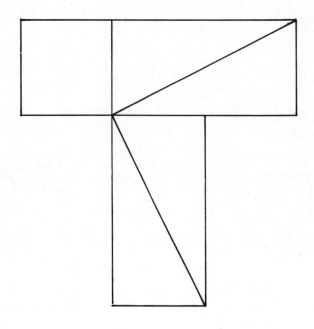

Maths puzzles

Copy the figure below on to a sheet of cardboard. Divide it into four parts of equal size and shape.

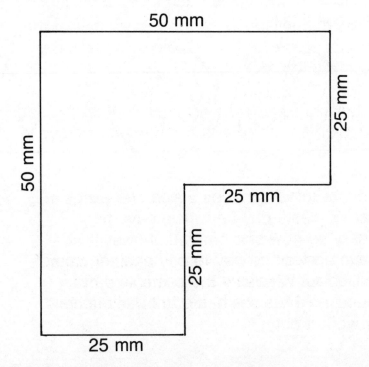

Draw the following patterns using one continuous line without crossing a line or lifting your pencil from the paper.

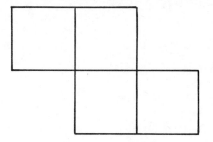

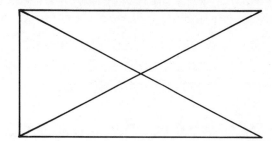

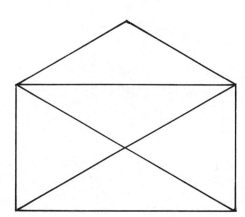

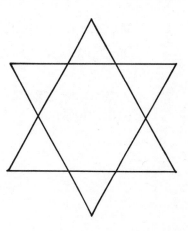

1   How many times does the digit 9 appear when writing the numbers from 1 to 100?

2   Put the numbers 1 to 10 into five pairs so that the total of each pair is 16, 7, 6, 17 and 9 (in that order). Use each number once only.

3   These four consecutive numbers 1, 2, 3 and 4 add up to 10. Which four consecutive numbers add up to 30?

4   What number, multiplied by 3 and divided by 4, is equal to 15.

5   Sue, John, Peter and Jill want to play a game of tennis doubles. What are the possible partner combinations? How many are there altogether?

Maths puzzles

1   Make two numbers using all the digits 1, 2, 3, 4, 5, 6, 7, 8 and 9 so that one of the numbers is twice as large as the other.

2   A clock loses 2½ minutes every hour. It reads the correct time at 2.00 pm. What time does it read the next day at 8.00 am?

3   What number leaves 6 if 8 is taken from half of it.

4   What are four consecutive odd numbers under 25 that add up to 80?

5   What are four consecutive numbers under 30 that total 94?

Maths puzzles

1   Keeping the order the same, make these digits equal to 100 exactly, by using $+ - \times$ and $\div$.

   1   2   3   4   5   6   7   8   9 = 100.

2   A pen and pencil cost 30 cents altogether. The pen cost 20 cents more than the pencil. How much did the pencil cost?

3   Make four 9s equal 100 exactly.

4   Sam is twice as old as Judi, but he is three years younger than Owen. What is Judi's age if Owen will be sixteen in two year's time?

5   What have these three numbers in common?

   36, 49 and 64.

Maths puzzles

1   For this puzzle you must use the numbers 1, 2, 3 and 4 only. Place one number in each box so that the box next to it holds a different number, ie a two can only touch a 1, 3 or 4 – till all the boxes are numbered using 1, 2, 3 and 4 over and over again.

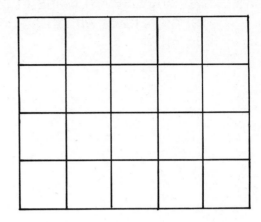

2   Insert the numbers 1, 2, 3, 4 ,5, 6 to this addition square so that the outer rows (across and down) add up to 18.

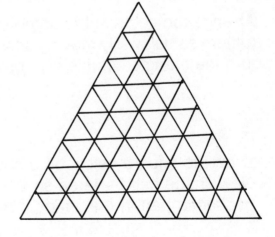

Maths puzzles

1   Look carefully at the diagram below. Can you find out how many triangles are in it?

2   The dots below are joined by five straight lines. Now join them using only four straight lines without lifting your pen off the paper.

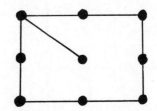

Maths puzzles

1 Arrange seven coins in five
   straight rows with three coins
   in each.

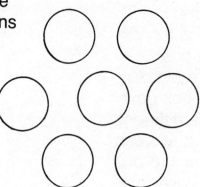

2 Farmer Jones has five mules and ten sections of
   steel fence. He wants to put each mule in a separate
   pen. Can you help him make five separate pens of
   equal size from the ten sections of fence?

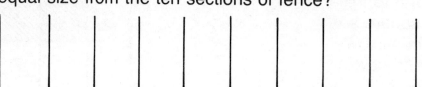

Maths puzzles

1 Arrange ten coins in the same triangle
   pattern as below. By moving only three coins
   turn the triangle completely upside down.

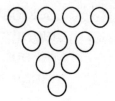

2 Draw the square below on a sheet of paper.
   Now shade half the area so there is an
   unshaded part in the shape of a square.

Maths puzzles

Copy the shape below onto a sheet of cardboard and cut it into the pieces shown. Shuffle the pieces and have someone time how long it takes you to arrange them into the original 'F' shape.

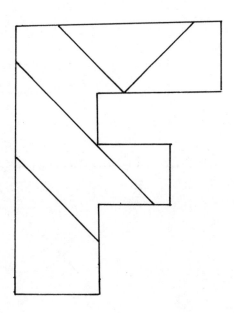

Maths puzzles

Copy the figure below onto a piece of cardboard and cut out the pieces as shown. Shuffle the pieces and rearrange them to form a square.

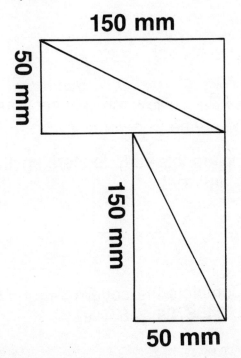

150 mm

50 mm

150 mm

50 mm

Draw the following patterns using one continuous line without crossing a line, retracing a line or lifting your pencil from the paper.

1

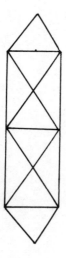

2

3

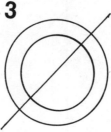

1   Multiply 143 by the digits from 1 to 9. When you have finished multiply each answer by 7 and check the results.

143 x 1,
143 x 2,
143 x 3
etc to 143 x 9.   Now multiply each answer by 7.

2   987654321
     − 123456789   Complete this sum. Is there anything peculiar about your answer?

3   a) 1 x 8
         b) 12 x 8
         c) 123 x 8

Complete the pattern through to
123456789 × 8 + 9 =

Observation and memory

Below are twenty common objects. Study them carefully for one minute, then cover the picture and see if you can write down the names of each one on a sheet of paper.

Observation and memory

Our artist was half asleep when he drew this picture. Can you spot at least fifteen mistakes he made? Write them on a piece of paper.

Observation and memory

The following are twenty words which students often find difficult to spell. Study the words carefully for three minutes, then cover them and see how many words you can remember and spell correctly. Write them on a sheet of paper.

library	always
school	Saturday
science	again
autumn	niece
February	separate
front	dairy
choir	awkward
blue	doctor
scissors	business
piece	through

Observation and memory

Study this picture for one minute, then cover it and answer the questions below on a sheet of paper.

1 What is the girl doing?
2 Which way is the wind blowing?
3 How many birds are there?
4 Who is standing on the path?

Observation and memory

Study these shapes very carefully. Work out how many cubes you would need to build each shape. Write your answers on a sheet of paper.

1

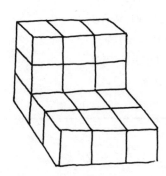

4

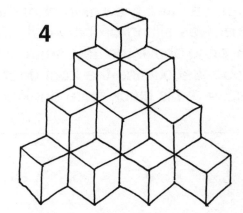

2

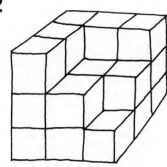

5

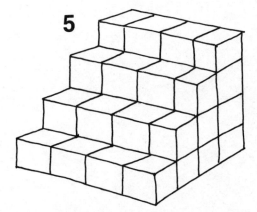

3

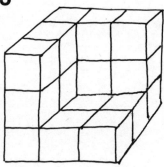

6

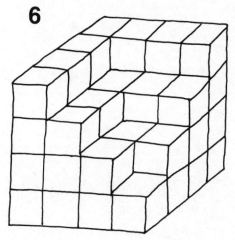

Observation and memory

Read this description of a country scene very carefully, then cover the paragraph and see if you can draw the scene from memory.

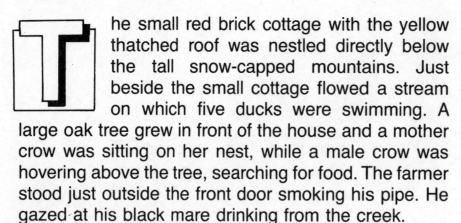

The small red brick cottage with the yellow thatched roof was nestled directly below the tall snow-capped mountains. Just beside the small cottage flowed a stream on which five ducks were swimming. A large oak tree grew in front of the house and a mother crow was sitting on her nest, while a male crow was hovering above the tree, searching for food. The farmer stood just outside the front door smoking his pipe. He gazed at his black mare drinking from the creek.

Below are fifteen different shapes. Study these shapes for one minute, then try to remember them all by drawing them on a sheet of paper.

Here are the portraits and names of six people. Study them for two minutes, then cover the left-hand side of the sheet and write the name of each person in picture on the right-hand side.

Belinda

Bob

Ben

Bill

Betty

Bonnie

Bill

Betty

Bob

Belinda

Ben

Bonnie

Study each of the questions below then write your answers on a sheet of paper.

1   In any open book, would page 137 be on the left or the right?

2   What two animals are featured on the back of a fifty-cent coin?

3   Are the numbers on a telephone dial arranged in order from 1 to 9 in a clockwise or anti-clockwise direction?

4   In the USA, does forward moving traffic keep to the left- or right-hand side of the road?

5   Does the Statue of Liberty in New York Harbour hold the flame in its left or right hand?

6   If you were to tear pages 8, 9, 47 and 48 out of a book, how many separate sheets of paper would you tear out?

Below are twelve common objects. Study them carefully for one minute, then cover the pictures and write down the names of each one on a piece of paper.

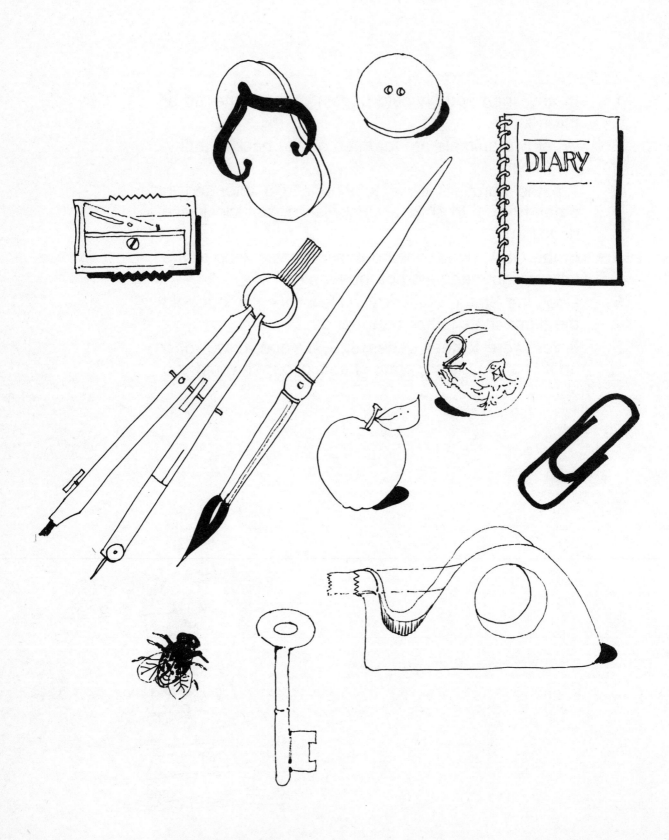

Observation and memory

Here is an assortment of shapes. Study them carefully for one minute, now cover them up and draw as many as you can on a sheet of paper.

A Guesstimate

Below are eight squares each containing a number of dots.
Look at each square individually, estimate the number of dots
and write your answer on a sheet of paper, then count the dots.
Compare your answers.

1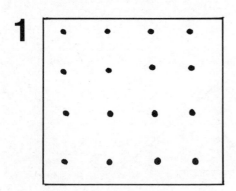

5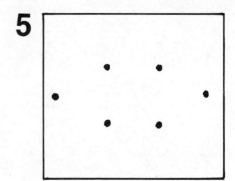

2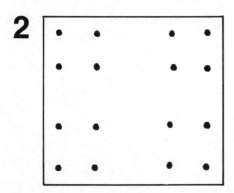

6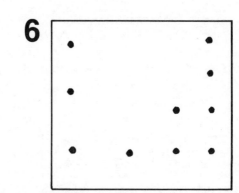

3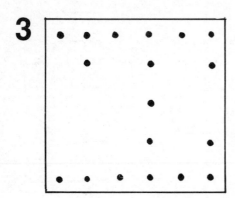

7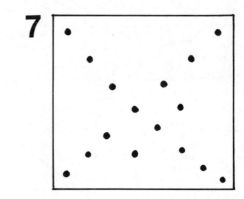

4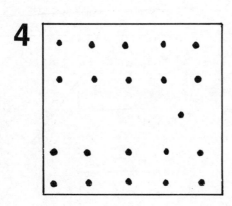

8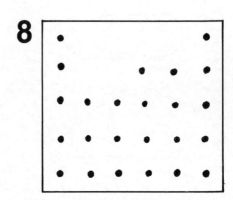

Observation and memory

Look carefully at these diagrams
and answer the questions without
using a ruler.

1   Which is the longer of the two
dotted lines?

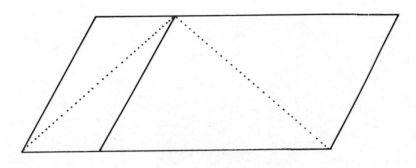

2   Which is the longer line, the
horizontal or the vertical?

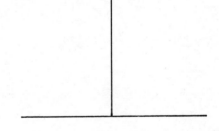

3   Which of these three lines is
the shortest?

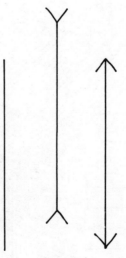

Observation and memory

Look carefully at the two pictures. In the second picture at least ten changes have been made. Can you find them?

Observation and memory

Study these shapes very carefully. Work out how many cubes you would need to build each shape. Write your answers on a sheet of paper.

1

4

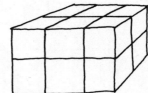

2

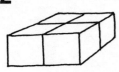

5

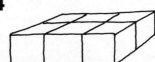

3

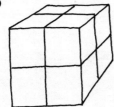

6

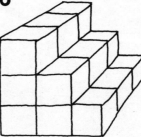

Study the picture carefully. Can you find at least ten things
that start with the letter 'p'?

Our artist wasn't feeling well when he drew this picture.
Can you spot at least ten mistakes he made? Write them
on a sheet of paper.

Shopping day

Nathan's mother went shopping at the supermarket. Here is her shopping list:

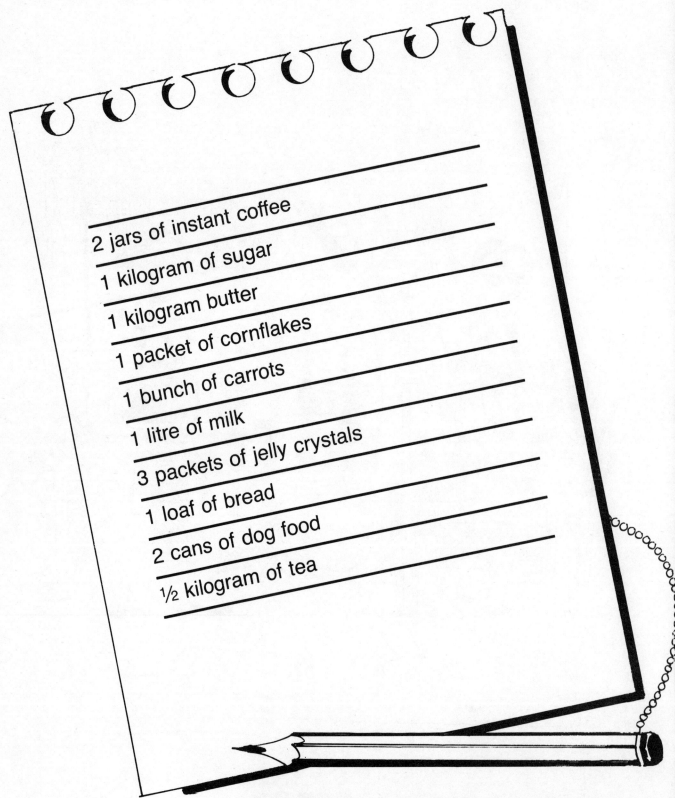

2 jars of instant coffee

1 kilogram of sugar

1 kilogram butter

1 packet of cornflakes

1 bunch of carrots

1 litre of milk

3 packets of jelly crystals

1 loaf of bread

2 cans of dog food

½ kilogram of tea

Study the list for one minute, then cover it up and write down all the items you can remember. Try also to remember the quantity of each item.

Test your eyes

Look carefully at the diagrams, then answer the questions without using a ruler. The following puzzles will test your ability to observe things carefully.

1 How does the distance AB compare with distance BC?

A   **B**   **C**

2 How many turns will the wheel make in rolling from A to B?

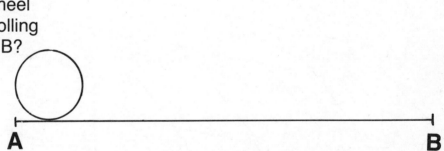

A   **B**

3 Which is the longer distance, AB or BC?

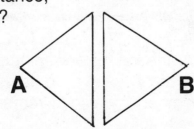 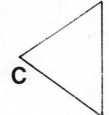

Observation and memory

Study these two pictures. In the second picture at least ten changes have been made. Can you spot them all?

General knowledge and vocabulary

1 Which of these words is spelled correctly (scissors, libary, Febuary).
2 The smallest continent in the world is (Asia, Europe, Australia).
3 Which word is out of place, (peach, apricot, radish, orange).
4 The first month which has thirty days is (April, May, March).
5 The tenth letter of the alphabet is (k, i, j).
6 Daffodils, violets, chrysanthemums are all types of (birds, insects, flowers).
7 A word that means the opposite of first is (good, last, old).
8 Which word in this group is a name for all the others (mosquito, insect, ant, bee, wasp)?
9 The number of days in a fortnight is (twelve, twenty-four, fourteen).
10 Christmas Day is on the (20th, 26th, 25th) of December.

General knowledge and vocabulary

1 The name for a group of insects is a (tuft, swarm, bundle).
2 Python, tiger and cobra are all types of (fish, butterflies, snakes).
3 An attic is a room (under, beside, above) a house.
4 A bat for tennis is called a (racquet, baton, javelin).
5 An animal like a large rabbit is a (hare, skunk, dingo).
6 Cider is made from (apples, lemons, grapes).
7 A eucalyptus is a type of (tree, dog, insect).
8 The world's highest mountain is (Washington, Everest, Kosciusko).
9 Which one of these is known as a citrus fruit (lemon, apricot, pear).
To listen to your heartbeat a doctor uses a (telescope, stethoscope, microscope).

General knowledge and vocabulary

1   An instrument for measuring temperature is a (barometer, thermometer, telescope).
2   A field in which fruit trees grow is called an (orchid, orchard, orchestra).
3   A soldier with three stripes on either arm is a (sergeant, private, captain).
4   The patron saint of Ireland is (St George, St Patrick, St Andrew).
5   The animal called the 'ship of the desert' is the (lion, horse, camel).
6   The capital city of New Zealand is (Dunedin, Wellington, Otago).
7   Which of these is a bird of prey (wren, magpie, eagle)?
8   An instrument that gives direction is a (turbine, theodolite, compass).
9   In what sport do you hear the terms 'greens', 'tees' and 'clubs'? (hockey, golf, badminton)?
10 How many players are there in a cricket team (eighteen, eleven, fifteen)?

General knowledge and vocabulary

1   The capital city of Japan is (Tokyo, Hiroshima, Nagasaki).
2   Which is not one of the primary colours (red, green, yellow)?
3   The smallest bird in the world is the (hummingbird, wren, robin).
4   A spider has (six, four, eight) legs.
5   The animal known as the 'king of beasts' is the (lion, tiger, zebra).
6   An instrument that attracts iron is a (meter, magnet, theodolite).
7   The home of a beaver is a (hutch, lodge, burrow).
8   South Africa is famous for its (diamonds, watches, emus).
9   Dirk Hartog was a famous (weightlifter, footballer, explorer).
10 In which of these years will an Olympic Games most likely be held (1992, 1998, 1994)?

General knowledge and vocabulary

1 A person who studies the stars is an (astronaut, astronomer, zoologist).
2 The fastest four-legged animal in the world is the (horse, greyhound, cheetah).
3 Ludwig Leichhardt was a famous (bushranger, musician, explorer).
4 The longest wall in the world is in (India, England, China).
5 A quadrilateral has (eight, three, four) sides.
6 The Mounties of Canada are famous (police, footballers, soldiers).
7 A carnivorous creature is one that eats (grass, meat, trees).
8 The city of Alice Springs is in (New South Wales, South Australia, Northern Territory).
9 Another name for a lift is an (elevator, escalator, entertainer).
10 Sir Donald Bradman was a famous (footballer, cricketer, swimmer).

General knowledge and vocabulary

Choose a word from the list to best complete each sentence.
1 Tuna, mullet and sardines are all types of _____ .
2 Mutton, venison and pork are all types of _____ .
3 Rice, wheat and oats are all types of _____ .
4 Alsatians, labradors and spaniels are all types of _____ .
5 Pacific, Indian, Arctic are all _____ .
6 Feathers are to birds as are to fish _____ .
7 Day is to week as month is to _____ .
8 The home of a horse is a _____ .
9 Silver, gold and iron are types of _____ .
10 Goannas, snakes and alligators are all _____ .

cereals fish oceans meat scales year dogs reptiles metals stable

General knowledge and vocabulary

Choose a word from the list to best complete each sentence

1   A word that means the opposite of dirty is _____ .
2   Television programs are copied on a _____ .
3   A word that means the same as empty is _____ .
4   What word below best completes this saying 'As white as _____ '.
5   Neck is to collar as wrist is to _____ .
6   The lady was presented with a _____ of flowers.
7   Venus, Saturn, Neptune are all _____ .
8   You would find an oven and refrigerator in the _____ .
9   Liquid used for washing dishes is called _____ .
10   The edge of a football oval is called the _____ .

vacant clean planets video detergent cuff bouquet snow kitchen boundary

---

General knowledge and vocabulary

Choose a word from the list to best complete each sentence.

1   A fertile place in the desert is an _____ .
2   The steps of a ladder are called the _____ .
3   A person who lives alone is called a _____ .
4   A period of ten years is a _____ .
5   A ship that travels below the ocean is a _____ .
6   A machine that makes electricity is called a _____ .
7   A place where birds are kept is an _____ .
8   The flesh of a sheep is called _____ .
9   A container for coins is a _____ .
10   A room on board a ship is called a _____ .

decade oasis mutton hermit submarine turbine purse aviary cabin rungs

General knowledge and vocabulary

Choose a word from the list to best complete each sentence.

1   A place for ice-skaters is a _____ .
2   The opposite to antique is _____ .
3   Another name for a donkey is _____ .
4   Another name for a moving staircase is an _____ .
5   A word which means the same as feeble is _____ .
6   A shoe with straps is called a _____ .
7   Plates, saucers, bowls are all pieces of _____ .
8   The record of a ship's progress is called a _____ .
9   Flock is to sheep as cattle is to _____ .
10 Cabbages, cauliflowers, broccoli are all types of _____ .

modern ass rink sandal escalator weak crockery log herd vegetables

---

General knowledge and vocabulary

Choose a word from the list to best complete each sentence.

1   The name for a period of one hundred years is a _____ .
2   Cypress, oak and beech are all types of _____ .
3   The meat of a deer is called _____ .
4   A stallion is a male _____ .
5   A word which means the same as residence is _____ .
6   A word which means the opposite of expand is _____ .
7   The young of a deer is called a _____ .
8   The home of a fox is called a _____ .
9   Complete 'As fresh as a _____ .'
10 A person who carries a golfer's clubs is a _____ .

venison century trees horse dwelling contract fawn den caddie daisy

General knowledge and vocabulary

Complete each word to make the name of a person who . . .
1   betrays his country – t_____ .
2   eats more than is good for him – g_____ .
3   is absent from school without permission – t_____ .
4   always looks on the bright side of things – o_____ .
5   hoards money – m_____ .
6   entertains people at his home – h_____ .
7   forsakes others to live entirely by himself – h_____ .
8   comes into our country to live – i_____ .
9   runs away from a fight – c_____ .
10 imitates the voices and actions of others – m_____ .

General knowledge and vocabulary

Give one word for the following. Their first letter is given to help you.
1   A doctor who performs operations – s_____ .
2   An instrument for telling directions – c_____ .
3   A breaking of a bone in the body – f_____ .
4   A place where chickens are hatched – i_____ .
5   Another name for a steed – h_____ .
6   A man who looks after sheep – s_____ .
7   A song for two people – d_____ .
8   A place where beer is made – b_____ .
9   The imaginary line running around the middle of the earth – e _____ .
10 A shallow crossing in a river – f_____ .

General knowledge and vocabulary   Activity 13

1   The unit of money used in France is (dollar, yen, franc).
2   Wolfgang Mozart was a famous (explorer, composer, inventor).
3   Clogs are worn by people of (Japan, South Africa, Holland).
4   The capital city of England is (Liverpool, London, Glasgow).
5   Ted is short for (William, Edward, Richard).
6   You are most likely to ride in a rickshaw in (Egypt, England, China).
7   The Statue of Liberty stands at the entrance to the harbour of (Paris, New York, London).
8   A rhododendron is a (flower, insect, animal).
9   The number of playing cards in a deck is (45, 52, 60).
10   Arteries are (blood vessels, sports, types of paintings).

General knowledge and vocabulary   Activity 14

1   Where on your body would you find a molar?
2   What part of your body would a chiropodist treat?
3   In what part of your body would you find a hammer and an anvil?
4   Citrus fruits, such as oranges and lemons, are important sources of what vitamin?
5   What is the common name for the spine?
6   What is the major function of your heart?
7   If a person had a nasal problem, what part of his body would be affected?
8   On what part of your body would you find a bunion or corn?
9   If you had dandruff, on what part of your body would you find it?
10   If you hit your 'funny bone', what part of your body would be hurt?

General knowledge and vocabulary

Name the occupations of the following.
1 A lady in charge of the nurses of a hospital.
2 A person who rides horses in races.
3 A person who handles deposits and withdrawals in a bank.
4 A person who cares for our teeth.
5 A person who sells medicines.
6 A person skilled in the use of herbs for treatment.
7 A person who writes for newspapers and magazines.
8 A person who travels for pleasure.
9 A person who investigates crime.
10 A person who designs buildings.

General knowledge and vocabulary

1 Fill in the missing words to complete this proverb – 'Birds of a
_____ flock _____'.
2 What is the name given to the footwear of the north American indians?
3 What person in our community would most likely own a kelpie?
4 For what do the initials USA stand?
5 What is the name given to large masses of ice found floating in the
Antarctic ocean?
6 Rearrange the letters of 'seaside' to get a word that means something
dangerous to man.
7 Peking is the capital of what country?
8 The largest Australian state in area is _____
9 For what was Neil Armstrong famous?
10 The acorn is the fruit of what tree?

General knowledge and vocabulary

1 A cygnet is a young (swan, eagle, signal).
2 Which planet in our solar system is farthest from the sun? (Pluto, Saturn, Mars).
3 The left-hand side of a ship is the (starboard, bow, port).
4 A gazebo is a (dwarf zebra, kind of summerhouse, a small antelope).
5 A sycamore is a type of (tree, dog, insect).
6 Khaki is a (fruit, colour, reptile).
7 On the back of a ten-cent coin is a (platypus, echidna, lyre-bird).
8 A turban is often worn by the people of (India, China, New Zealand).
9 One of the wind instruments of an orchestra is a (violin, piano, trumpet).
10 Which one of these words is spelled incorrectly (admission, scissors, orphen).

General knowledge and vocabulary

Give one word for:
1 Soldiers on horseback.
2 The middle part of an apple.
3 A person who eats no meat.
4 A place where fish are kept.
5 A vessel for holding flowers.
6 A container for paper money.
7 A person who travels on foot.
8 An unmarried man.
9 A child whose parents are dead.
10 The name given to a substance which can kill you.

General knowledge and vocabulary

1 Brisbane is the capital city of (Queensland, Victoria, Tasmania).
2 Which is Australia's highest mountain (Feathertop, Kosciusko, Buffalo)?
3 Henry Lawson was a famous (poet, inventor, doctor).
4 A Karri is a species of Australian (lizard, tree, shellfish).
5 Australia's largest city is (Melbourne, Perth, Sydney).
6 Which of these animals is a marsupial (kangaroo, dingo, alligator).
7 Ben Hall was a famous (author, bushranger, disc jockey).
8 What creature is featured on the back of a one-cent coin (lyre-bird, platypus, echidna).
9 The smallest Australian state in area is (Victoria, Tasmania, Western Australia).
10 Digger was the name given to (soldiers, footballers, drovers).

General knowledge and vocabulary

1 What is the name given to where earth and sky meet?
2 Give another name for daybreak.
3 What do we call pieces of fish from which bones have been removed?
4 What is the name given to a room beneath a house?
5 By what four-letter word is molten rock known?
6 The name given to a religious song.
7 What word beginning with 't' means a machine that makes electricity?
8 What is the name for the bony structure of your body?
9 What word beginning with 'a' means a hired killer?
10 What is the six-letter word that names a place where aeroplanes are kept?

Teasers and logical puzzles

1 How can you make an odd number like seven even?
2 What is found in the middle of both America and Australia?
3 Alan decided to paint his new bicycle red and to give it three coats of paint. Which coat will be put on the first?
4 What is in the middle of Paris?
5 Why do white sheep in Australia eat more than black sheep?

Teasers and logical puzzles

1 What occurs once in a minute, twice in a moment yet not at all in a week?
2 On a piece of paper write the word 'to'. Now write 'too' and then write the number 'two'. Now write the second day of the week.
3 How much soil can be removed from a hole two metres deep, two metres long and two metres wide?
4 A farmer had twenty ducks and all but eleven died. How many has he left?
5 Which of the following is correct:
Twelve nines are one hundred and seven.
or
Twelve nines is one hundred and seven.

Teasers and logical puzzles

All of the following questions have a catch, so be careful.

1   Count from ten to one backwards. Write your answer on a sheet of paper.

2   To what question can you truthfully answer nothing but 'yes'?

3   Read this, then write it correctly on a piece of paper. to, -ot, h -a - c, he - s

4   How long will an eight-day clock go without winding?

5   What continents are south of the North Pole?

Teasers and logical puzzles

1   In front of a saloon in the wild west was a post with a board attached to it. It read:

T O T I

E M U L

E S T O

Can you explain what the post was used for?

2   A crafty coin dealer tried to sell some coins to a keen coin collector. All the coins were dated 57 BC. Do you think the coin collector would be getting a bargain?

3   A large ship moored to the jetty has a rope ladder hanging over its side. Each rung of the ladder is 2 cm in diameter and the rungs are 50 cm apart, centre to centre. The ladder hangs down to the water, the water just covering the fifth rung from the bottom. If the tide rises at a uniform rate of 10 cm per hour, how many rungs will be submerged after two hours? A drawing might help you find the answer.

Teasers and logical puzzles

1   Bruno is going duck-shooting and has a boat on top of his car. However, the car becomes jammed in the door of his garage. It only needs a centimetre or two to free it again. He does not want to take the boat off. What should Bruno do?

2   It is a dark night and you are making your way through the desert by torchlight. An insect flies into your ear. It is too deep for you to reach and naturally you are a long way from a doctor. What could you do to get the insect out?

3   Melanie goes to the shop to get the newspaper and an ice-cream on a stick. She returns to her house and finds her flat-mate has locked the door from the inside. He is fast asleep and she does not want to wake him. It is an old type lock, and she looks in the keyhole to see the large key is in it. What should Melanie do?

Teasers and logical puzzles

1   A cat goes into a barn with four legs and later appears with eight. Can you explain this?

2   What famous English captain visited Australia but was never able to play in a test match?

3   A scientist made an amazing discovery. He invented a liquid so powerful that it would dissolve any substance known on Earth. He made millions of dollars selling it for $15 a bottle. Can you explain the flaw in this story?

4   Study this word carefully: NOON
    Can you work out what is strange about it apart from it being spelled the same forwards and backwards? If you do discover what is strange about it see if you can work out some more words the same and write them down.

Teasers and logical puzzles

1   If a plane crashed into the centre of the Murray River, which forms the border between NSW and Victoria in which state would they bury the survivors?

2   Peter and Judy were neighbours. One day Peter's peacock flew into Judy's yard and laid an egg on the lawn. Judy claimed the egg as her own because it was laid on her property. Peter objected strongly. Who do you think owns the egg?

3   One day Billy, a boy of doubtful character, was caught red-handed with a bag of freshly-picked peanuts. Billy denied stealing them. He, in fact, claimed a strong wind had blown the ripe ones off the branches of the peanut tree onto the road-side and therefore they could be picked up by anyone. The policeman immediately arrested him for he did not believe his story. Why?

Teasers and logical puzzles

1   Peter and Susan are left at home by themselves while their parents go shopping. While they are playing in the kitchen they begin to throw a cricket ball to each other. Peter misses the ball and it breaks the large glass window and lands on the lawn outside. The terrified children decide upon a cunning plan to fool their parents.

2   They hide the cricket ball and get a rock from the garden and put it on the lino of the kitchen. When their parents arrive home the children tell their dad that some unknown person in the street threw a stone through the window. The father immediately punishes them for breaking the window and telling lies. Explain how the father knew the children were lying.

3   Julie was participating in a particular sport. During the afternoon she won four races yet at no time did she cross the finishing line. What sport was she taking part in?

4   A man was blindfolded and then someone hung up his hat. Rifle in hand, the man walked fifty paces, turned around and shot a hole through his hat. Can you explain how this was possible?

Teasers and logical puzzles

1   One day Sam travelled from Wagga to Adelaide in his new sports car. On the entire journey one of his tyres was constantly flat yet at no time did he realise this, although he was travelling at high speed for much of the journey. Can you explain why?

2   A farmer has five eggs for his lunch every day, but does not keep any fowls or chickens on his farm. He does not buy, borrow, steal or beg the eggs, and no-one gives him any. How then does he manage to have five eggs for lunch each day?

3   When Ross joined the police force everyone agreed that the people would now be better protected. Ross was liked by all his workmates mainly because he never complained even though he often worked very long hours. He was extremely competent and enjoyed his work a great deal. In spite of this good work Ross never received a salary and was never promoted even though he served the force well for many years before retiring. Can you give the reason for this?

Teasers and logical puzzles

1   At a seaside resort there had been many drownings because of the treacherous tides. However the responsible people of the community decided to prevent any more tragedies. To do this they erected a sign in the ocean that read: DO NOT SWIM IN THIS AREA WHEN THIS SIGN IS UNDERWATER The drownings, however, continued. Can you explain why?

2   A drawer contains 12 socks, six red and six blue. If it is dark and you have no light, how many socks will you have to take out of the drawer to be sure of getting either a pair of red or a pair of blue socks?

3   One day a boy was dozing in school. He dreamt that he had been caught by a savage horde of natives and was about to be executed. Just as the witchdoctor was about to bring the axe down on his head in his dream the boy sitting in the desk behind leant over and touched the dreamer on the back of the neck. The dreaming boy got such a fright he died instantly. Do you know why this story could not possibly be true?

Teasers and logical puzzles

1. What is pig skin mainly used for?
2. In how many years during the century do Christmas Day and New Year's Day fall in the same year?
3. What months have twenty-eight days?
4. Rearrange the letter of the two words below to make one word. NEW DOOR
5. How many times can you subtract 3 from 24?

Teasers and logical puzzles

1. Complete this pattern:
   O T T F F S S E
2. Write this number in figures:
   Eleven thousand eleven hundred and eleven
3. I have two Australian coins in my pocket. Their total value is fifteen cents. One is not a five-cent piece. What are the coins?
4. Divide 30 by ½ and add 5. What is your answer?
5. How far can you travel along the Equator before going west?

Teasers and logical puzzles

1   If a doctor gives his patient three pills to take and says to take one every half hour, how long will the pills last?

2   Is a man able to marry his widow's sister? If not, why?

3   If Sam's father is Michael's son, what relation is Sam to Michael.

4   Complete this pattern: u o i e

5   If yesterday fortnight was a Friday, what is tomorrow?

Teasers and logical puzzles

1   A bear hunter left his camp and walked two kilometres south. He then walked one kilometre east where he shot a bear. He then walked two kilometres north and found himself back at his camp. I knew then that the bear was white. Why?

2   A cheeky young lad, after having his hair cut, turned to the barber and said, 'Right, I'll have my ice-cream now.' 'What do you mean?' said the barber.
'Well you have a sign at the front window which reads *What do you think? I'll cut your hair for nothing and buy you an ice-cream!*' 'Oh no!' replied the barber. 'My silly assistant put the punctuation marks in the wrong place.' Can you explain how the barber should have punctuated the sign?

3   Farmer Jones once noticed a group of school children in the paddock in which he kept his cows. He noticed there were twice as many children as cows. When he counted feet and heads he found there was a total of 99 heads and feet in the paddock. How many children and how many cows were there in the paddock?

Teasers and logical puzzles

1   It is an extremely black night on a lonely deserted road and your car has a puncture in the front wheel. You begin to remove the flat tyre carefully placing the nuts in the wheel cap. However, while you are not looking your two-year-old child picks up the wheel nuts and scatters them away from the car. You have no torch or matches, and as it is sandy, you do not wish to rummage around for fear of burying the nuts in the sand. What could you do to find the nuts?

2   A garage once received a call from a motorist in distress. The repair truck that attended found the motorist standing beside his car, the engine was running smoothly and there was no outward signs of disrepair to the car. A little while later the car in distress returned to the garage, towing the tow truck. Can you determine what was wrong with the car?

3   You are a sailor and during heavy seas your ship sinks. You swim to a deserted island on which there is no wood. You find a lamp which you can use to signal a passing ship. However, there is only about three centimetres of oil in the lamp – not enough to reach the wick. What would you do?

Teasers and logical puzzles

1   Recently in the local newspaper there was a report of a dreadful crime. A life had been taken and even though the police knew the whereabouts of the person who had committed the crime they would not arrest him. Do you know why?

2   To become president of West Krypton the constitution specifies four requirements.

These are:
1 The candidate must be at least fifty years of age.
2 The candidate must have been born in West Krypton.
3 The candidate must have lived in West Krypton all his life.

What is the fourth requirement?

Teasers and logical puzzles

1. In 'The Shriekers' pop group three of its members can play the guitar and four of them can sing, two of them play and sing, one can do neither, two can sing only and one can play only. How many members are there in the group?

2. Tommy was given one dollar a month by his father to spend. However the boy was not satisfied and asked his dad could he change his allowance. His proposal was for his dad to give him one cent for January, two cents for February, four cents for March etc, twice as much each month until the end of the year. Can you explain if the boy would have been better or worse off?

3. Can you explain what is wrong with this tombstone, found in an old gold mining town in New South Wales? 'Here lies Joe Jones who died of starvation on 18th November 1865. Aged 73 years. And also his widow Martha who died of tuberculosis on 16th February, 1851. Aged 52 years.'

Teasers and logical puzzles

1. A man from the city was making his first trip to the country. He decided to travel from Kerang to a little place called Woorinen to see a farmer friend. However after travelling some considerable distance from Kerang he came to a crossroad. Unfortunately the signpost had fallen down. On closer inspection, he found that the signs pointed in four different directions. One pointed to Woorinen, one to Tyntynder, one to Nyah and one to Kerang. Can you explain how the city man worked out which road led him to Woorinen?

2. A tramp collected cigarette butts. From every four butts he finds he can make one cigarette. If he finds sixteen butts how many cigarettes can he have?

3. 'More people in Wagga win the lottery than in any other city in the state of New South Wales', said John. 'We are therefore going to live in Wagga, so we will have a better chance of winning the big prizes than if we stayed here in our little country town,' continued John. Explain if John's reasoning was sound.

Teasers and logical puzzles

1   Michael was playing in an important professional golf championship when, after a beautiful drive, his ball came to rest in the middle of a brown paper bag left on the course by an untidy spectator. As the golfer was only one stroke off the lead and had a good chance of winning the first prize of $50,000, he did not wish to be penalised a stroke for picking up the ball. Can you suggest the simplest thing for him to do?

2   Peter and Pat are twins. Pat has twice as many brothers as sisters, and Peter has the same number of brothers and sisters. Explain how many children there are in the family.

3   The number of plums in a case doubled every minute. The pickers started with an empty case at exactly 10.29 am and the case was full at 11·00 am. Can you tell at what time the case was half full?

4   Once I met an old man who told of many experiences during his life. He had been an explorer in Africa, a goldminer in Australia and even served five years as a lieutenant in the Swiss navy. Explain why I shouldn't believe this old man's tales?

Teasers and logical puzzles

1   Two children are born to the same mother on the same date, in the same year within a few moments of each other yet they are not twins. How can this be?

2   What was the Prime Minister's name in 1964?

3   Read the following then write what each says.
(i) RU sure K8 her p p p?
(ii) Don't tttbbb
(iii) Y Y U R Y Y U B I C U R Y Y 4 me
(iv) O I C U R M T

Games for two or three

Draw a grid as for noughts and crosses. One player uses the odd numbers to 9 (13579). The other player uses the even numbers to 8 (02468). One player begins by putting one of his numbers in a square, and is followed by his opponent. Each number can only be used once and each player is allowed to use only his numbers. The winner is the first player to form a line of three numbers totalling fifteen.

Games for two or three

Each player takes ten beans (pieces of chalk or stones will do.) Hiding your hand behind your back, put either an odd or even number of beans in your hand. You then present this closed hand to your opponent who tries to guess the number, after being told it is either an odd or an even number. If your opponent guesses correctly he takes all the beans. If he is wrong he must give the 'holding' player the difference between the guess and the number in his hand. The opponent then presents an odd or even number in his hand and you must guess. The game continues until one player has all the beans.

Games for two or three

Draw the grid below on a sheet of paper. Take turns placing sticks or going over lines with a coloured pencil. Whenever a player completes a square enter that player's initial in the square. Then that player takes another turn. The winner is the player with the most initials entered.

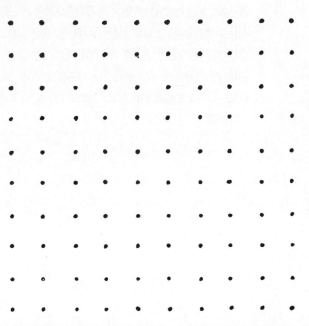

Games for two or three

This time two people play each other at noughts and crosses but a third person records each move, ie the two people face away from the recorder and name the position they want one after the other, eg middle left, top right, bottom left etc. The first person who gets three in a row is the winner as with ordinary noughts and crosses.

Games for two or three

Play noughts and crosses with your partner – with one big difference. The person who gets three noughts or crosses in a row is the loser.

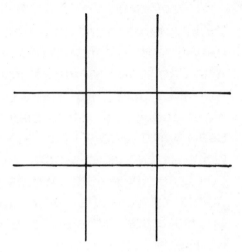

Games for two or three

Make four rows of matches as set out below.

```
        |
      | | |
    | | | | |
  | | | | | | |
```

Now take turns removing from one to three matches from any one row. The loser is the person to pick up the very last stick.

Write a large word on a sheet of paper. Now in three minutes see who can make the most smaller words by using the letters of the word. Individual letters may not be used twice. Score by giving one point for two-letter words, two points for three-letter words, three points for four-letter words and so on. Here are some suitable words to use:

ARITHMETIC
HALLOWEEN
GENERATION
DEPENDABILITY
PARENTS
MAGISTRATE
NATIONALITY
CONGLOMERATION

Get a large sheet of paper. One player writes a word across the page starting on the top left hand part of the paper. His opponent then writes a word that begins with the last letter of the word which was written. Each player receives one point for each letter of the word.

```
e l e p h a n t
              e
              n
              n
              i
      s p a r r o w
```

This game begins by one person writing or saying a word. His opponent then makes a word beginning with the last letter of the preceding word. However for this game, each word must be an animal or object which has four legs. Words can simply be said or written after each other, eg rat, table, elephant, trestle, elk, kid, etc.

The players sit around and one tosses a duster or bean bag across to another, at the same time calling out a word of three letters, eg cat, and immediately beginning to count up to twelve, finishing – 'eleven, twelve, Chop'. The one who receives the toss tries, before 'Chop' is said, to reply with three words each beginning with one of the letters of the original word in their proper order, eg for CAT the words might be CLOWN, APPLE, TENT. When the reply is given in time the successful player throws to someone else, but if he fails and 'Chop' cuts him short, he falls out of the game. Thus eventually only one player is left.

ANSWERS

Left-out letters   ACTIVITY 1

A

1 pencil, **2** hollow, bellow, fellow etc, **3** prison, **4** tennis, **5** wicket, bucket, packet etc, **6** planet, **7** escape, **8** orange, arrange, **9** engine

B

1 donkey, **2** needle, **3** silver, **4** blonde, **5** rabbit, **6** centre, **7** purple **8** stupid, **9** dahlia, **10** cattle **11** ballad, **12** tunnel

---

Anagrams   ACTIVITY 2

A

1 table **2** cheap, **3** march, **4** owl, **5** raw, **6** wolf, **7** heart, **8** finger, **9** horse

B

1 mean, mane, **2** meat, mate, team, **3** read, dear, **4** tide, diet, **5** limes, miles, **6** rail, liar, **7** meal, male, **8** priest, stripe, **9** care, race

---

Making Words   ACTIVITY 3

A Answers will vary

B Answers will vary,

samples are: bear, mouse, lion, moose, cat, dog, goat, horse, doe, tiger

---

Word pieces   ACTIVITY 4

A

1 nomad, **2** shorthand, **3** hostage, **4** rampage, **5** attack, **6** reappear, **7** pattern, **8** cartridge, **9** bracelet

B

1 kill slaughter, **2** pie tart, **3** rip tear, **4** one single, **5** shed barn, **6** boat ship, **7** cut slash, **8** bare bald

---

Missing letters   ACTIVITY 5

A

1 please, **2** fleece, **3** steel, **4** tree, **5** eleven, **6** eagle, **7** every or very, **8** green, **9** coffee, **10** jewel, **11** cheese, **12** fence

B

1 shirt, **2** film, **3** finish, **4** skipping, **5** knife, **6** ship, **7** dirty, **8** direction, **9** spirit, **10** silver, **11** said, **12** police

---

Jumbled words   ACTIVITY 6

A

1 drum, **2** best, **3** hope, **4** cart, **5** thin, **6** shut, **7** help, **8** draw, **9** load, **10** ugly

Missing vowels

B

1 kookaburra, **2** kiwi, **3** sparrow, **4** parrot, **5** flamingo, **6** vulture, **7** budgerigar, **8** peacock, **9** pelican, **10** thrush

---

Word pieces   ACTIVITY 7

A

1 knife alone, **2** table snake, **3** would money, **4** burst coast, **5** music brush, **6** dirty again, **7** dozen cliff, **8** chair match, **9** prize toast, **10** quick every

B

1 picnic afraid, **2** island fellow, **3** purple animal, **4** follow season, **5** during twelve, **6** corner heaven, **7** engine narrow, **8** nature silver, **9** museum pigeon, **10** bridge bundle,

---

ACTIVITY 8

'Cat' words

A

1 catamaran, **2** cathedral, **3** catechism, **4** catastrophe, **5** catalogue, **6** catapult, **7** cattle, **8** caterpillar, **9** cataract, **10** catnap

'Car' words

B

1 caribou, **2** carnivorous, **3** cartoon, **4** caravan, **5** carbine or cartridge, **6** cardigan, **7** carnation, **8** carrot, **9** carpet, **10** carafe

---

ACTIVITY 9

Hidden words

A

1 lead, **2** nickel, **3** ruby, **4** iron, **5** opal, **6** tin, **7** steel, **8** gold, **9** silver, **10** zinc

B

1 wasp, **2** gnat, **3** aphid, **4** hornet, **5** louse, **6** weevil, **7** locust, **8** earwig, **9** flea, **10** moth

---

ACTIVITY 10

Hidden Birds

A

1 plover, **2** comorant, **3** ostrich, **4** chicken, **5** swallow, **6** thrush, **7** sparrow or crow, **8** pelican or toucan, **9** magpie

B

1 swallow, **2** puffin, **3** starling, **4** robin, **5** ibis, **6** eagle, **7** hawk, **8** heron

---

ACTIVITY 11

Back-to-front words

A

1 husband, **2** beautiful, **3** writing, **4** chocolate, **5** tomatoes, **6** electric, **7** ribbon, **8** vegetable, **9** balloon, **10** always

Stars and stripes

B

1 scone, muffin **2** petrol, gasoline **3** holiday, vacation **4** lollies, candy **5** luggage, baggage **6** timetable, schedule **7** footpath, sidewalk **8** soft drink, soda-pop **9** car, automobile **10** tram, street-car

---

ACTIVITY 12

Dropping letters

A

1 tore, **2** four, **3** chap, **4** lather, **5** hair, **6** seal, **7** caves, **8** heat, **9** spar, **10** hoe

Adding letters

B

1 tally, **2** modest, **3** gully, **4** camel, **5** stampede, **6** cameo, **7** yearn, **8** stingy, **9** grime, **10** hearth

---

ACTIVITY 13

Missing letters

A

1 glove, **2** hotel, **3** dairy, **4** dirty, **5** forty, **6** snail, **7** truck, **8** leave, **9** melon, **10** torch

Hidden words

B

1 porpoise, **2** platypus, **3** python, **4** lizard, **5** reindeer, **6** hamster, **7** piranha, **8** pelican, **9** flamingo, **10** buffalo

Animal mysteries
ACTIVITY 14

A

1 cheetah, **2** elephant, **3** buffalo, **4** baboon, **5** gorilla, **6** hedgehog, **7** giraffe, **8** ferret, **9** mongoose, **10** squirrel

One word for many

B

1 tree, **2** tool, **3** meat, **4** bird, **5** fruit, **6** colour, **7** furniture, **8** metal, **9** vegetable, **10** fish

Puzzling words
ACTIVITY 15

A

1 falling stars **2** Lost in the forest **3** Long overdue **4** I'm fed up **5** Look around you

B

Self-correcting

Fruits
ACTIVITY 16

lemon, orange, pear, tomato, fig, apple, mango, plum, banana, peach, cherry, apricot, lime, quince, olive

Body parts
ACTIVITY 17

skeleton, jaw, liver, arms, eyes, toes, knee, neck, mouth, tongue, skin, skull, heart, ribs, wrist, beard, hair, elbow, ear, teeth

Colours
ACTIVITY 18

orange, green, white, brown, red, yellow, black, fawn, grey, purple, pink, gold, blue, cream

Clothing
ACTIVITY 19

scarf, sandal, tie, dress, smock, skirt, pyjamas, gloves, vest, sock, coat, shirt, frock, beret, cap, apron, hat, belt, suit, trousers

Inside the home
ACTIVITY 20

cupboard, saucer, mirror, sofa, curtain, lamp, oven, basin, carpet, radio, stove, spoon, frypan, rug, knife, telephone

Left-out letters
ACTIVITY 21

A

1 applaud, **2** mistake, **3** village, **4** holiday, **5** station, **6** petunia, **7** climate, **8** blossom, **9** address, **10** blanket

B

1 wonderful, **2** chocolate, **3** cathedral, **4** chauffeur, **5** albatross, **6** marmalade, **7** telephone, **8** exhausted, **9** hilarious, **10** mannequin

Anagrams
ACTIVITY 22

A

1 signed, singed, design; **2** silent, tinsel, listen, inlets; **3** stop, pots, post, spot; **4** lemons, melons; **5** steal, stale, tales, slate; **6** rates, stare, tears; **7** disease; **8** same, seam; **9** wines, sinew; **10** tablet.

Add-a-word anagrams

B

1 beach, **2** butler, **3** shirt, **4** scare, **5** bread, **6** feast, **7** certain, **8** silent

Making words # ACTIVITY 23
A
Self-correcting.
Fruit Salad
B

fig, cherry, guava, lime, apricot, raisin, pear, plum, mango, avocado

---

A # ACTIVITY 24
1 satisfactory, **2** attendant, **3** lieutenant, **4** candidate, **5** forgotten, **6** innocent, **7** together, **8** noticeable
B
1 save, salvage, **2** store, mart, **3** spin, gyrate, **4** brawl, fight, **5** hovel, shack, **6** face, front, **7** store, save, **8** arch, dome

---

Missing letters # ACTIVITY 25
A
1 fold, flood, **2** chocolate, **3** cord, **4** voice, **5** cotton, **6** soup, **7** blossom, **8** choose, chose, **9** famous, **10** cough
B
1 cabbage, **2** balloon, **3** problem, **4** break, **5** library, **6** probably, **7** bubble, **8** double, **9** mobile, **10** goblet

---

Jumbled words # ACTIVITY 26
A
1 tiger, **2** pansy, **3** throw, **4** honey, **5** habit, **6** zebra, **7** glass, **8** camel, **9** found, **10** giant
Missing consonants
B
1 golf, **2** tennis, **3** cricket, **4** skiing, **5** hockey or soccer, **6** softball, **7** bowling, **8** chess, **9** rowing, **10** athletics

---

Word make # ACTIVITY 27
A
1 stable bucket, **2** ticket splash, **3** moment church, **4** pocket cattle, **5** cheese should, **6** summer branch, **7** silver stable, **8** button police
B
1 honeymoon kilograms, **2** orchestra sculpture, **3** orchestra collector, **4** imaginary secretary, **5** orphanage sculpture, **6** discovery emergency, **7** gymnasium hibernate, **8** casserole vegetable

---

'Ant' words # ACTIVITY 28
A
1 elephant, **2** anthem, **3** antique, **4** anthology, **5** antler
'Art' words
B
1 start, **2** chart, **3** heart, **4** artificial, **5** artery

ACTIVITY 29

Hidden words
A
1 banana, **2** lemon, **3** orange, **4** apple, **5** mango, **6** tomato, **7** lychees,
8 pear, **9** quince, **10** peach
B
1 beef, **2** bread, **3** lamb, **4** salt, **5** mustard, **6** butter, **7** stew, **8** cream,
9 cereal, **10** pear

ACTIVITY 30

A
1 wombat, **2** elephant, **3** whale, **4** bison, **5** wallaby, **6** goat, **7** rabbit, **8** monkey,
donkey, turkey, **9** porcupine, **10** possum
B
1 rabbit, **2** camel, **3** beaver, **4** swan, **5** snail

ACTIVITY 31

Hidden females
A
1 sow, **2** doe, **3** ewe, **4** cow, **5** goose
Changing words
B
1 pamper,
2 dedication, **3** gloat, **4** brawl, **5** rubble

ACTIVITY 32

Time for a change
A
1 pillage, **2** furrow, **3** kilt, **4** durable, **5** baffle
Getting ahead
B
1 swarm, **2** stow, **3** sheath, **4** ebony, **5** glisten

ACTIVITY 33

Centre pieces
A
1 parent, **2** pickle, **3** pencil, **4** parade, **5** palace, **6** pastry, **7** people, **8** parrot,
9 picnic, **10** poetry
Two-in-one crossout
B
1 magpie cricket, **2** hornet beagle, **3** sugar hermit, **4** pyjamas pyramid

ACTIVITY 34

Tricky vowels
A
1 numerous, **2** fatigue, **3** realise, **4** scholar, **5** hygiene, **6** spectacle,
7 emphasis, **8** prodigy, **9** felony, **10** custody
Out-of-place words
B
1 siamese, **2** plough, **3** chess, **4** optimist, **5** window, **6** sailor, **7** apricot, **8** serial

ACTIVITY 35

Drop-a-letter
A
(i) startling – starling, staring, string, sting, sing, sin, in, I **(ii)** Therein – there,
the, rein, in, her, herein, ere, here, he, I

Special words

B

1 Has all the vowels in order
2 Has six vowels, all 'i'
3 Has three dotted letters in a row
4 Begins with a consonant followed by four vowels
5 Has three consecutive sets of double letters
6 Has eight letters and only one vowel

Colours   **ACTIVITY 36**

emerald, sepia, cerise, sienna, mauve, magenta, khaki, beige, copper, maroon, lime, amber, rust, rose, auburn, turquoise

---

Animals   **ACTIVITY 37**

giraffe, deer, seal, skunk, gorilla, bison, elk, ape, otter, lion, baboon, rabbit, puma, camel, bear, ferret, polecat, beaver, fox, mouse

---

Sports   **ACTIVITY 38**

archery, rowing, tennis, athletics, diving, judo, rugby, golf, hiking, skiing, sailing, cricket, polo, hockey, boxing

---

Birds   **ACTIVITY 39**

eagle, thrush, kiwi, crow, albatross, buzzard, woodpecker, dove, curlew, emu, duck, wagtail, ibis, owl, robin, raven, hawk, lark, wren, swan

---

Occupations   **ACTIVITY 40**

architect, surgeon, butcher, pilot, apiarist, typist, actor, plumber, publisher, shearer, ranger, jockey, translator, teacher, chef, surveyor

Maths Puzzles

     ACTIVITY 1

1 4,5,6,7
2 a) $3 \times 3 + 10 = 19$ b) $9 + 3 \div 6 = 2$
   c) $7 - 7 \times 6 = 0$ d) $8 - 3 \div 5 = 1$
3 4 **4** 12 **5** they are all odd numbers

     ACTIVITY 2

1 18 (9 pairs) **2** 10 **3** 45 **4** 32 **5** six dozen dozen = 864.
Half-a-dozen = 72. Difference = 792.

     ACTIVITY 3

1

2	9	4
7	5	3
6	1	8

2

```
        (2)
     (8)   (9)
   (4)       (5)
 (3) (6) (7) (1)
```

ACTIVITY 4

1 At least 33 rectangles

2

ACTIVITY 5

1 Place the bottom coin on top of the first.

2

ACTIVITY 6

1 Invert the outside coins three times.

2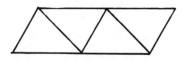

ACTIVITY 7

Self-correcting

ACTIVITY 8

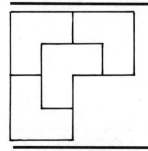

ACTIVITY 9

Self-correcting

ACTIVITY 10

1 20 times **2** 6 + 10, 4 + 3, 1 + 5, 8 + 9, 2 + 7 **3** 6,7,8,9 **4** 20 **5** 3

ACTIVITY 11

1 13 458 and 6729 **2** 7.15 am **3** 28 **4** 17,19,21,23 **5** 22,23,24,25

ACTIVITY 12

1 $1 + 2 + 3 + 4 + 5 + 6 + 7 + (8 \times 9) = 100$ **2** The pencil cost 5 cents
3 $99 \frac{9}{9} = 100$ **4** 5½ years **5** They are all square numbers

ACTIVITY 13

1

1	2	3	4	3
3	4	1	2	1
1	2	3	4	3
3	4	1	2	1

(other combinations are possible)

2

5	8	3	2
9			10
4	1	7	6

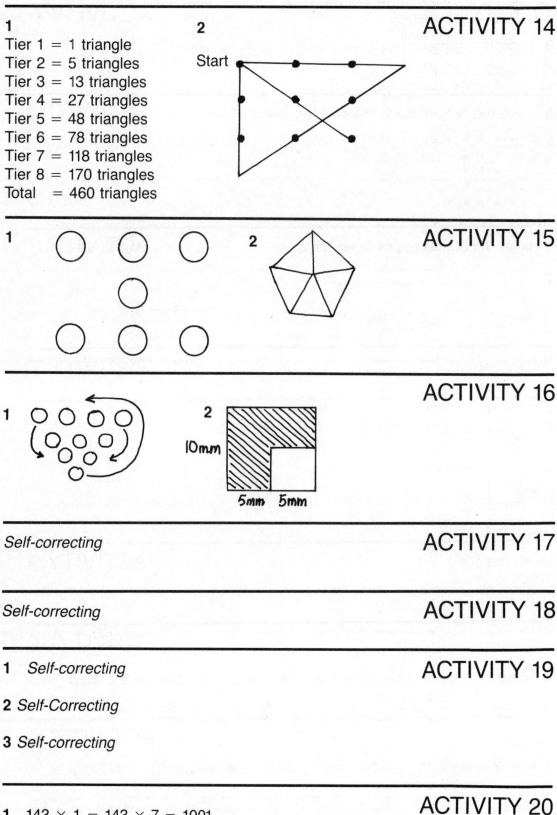

ACTIVITY 14

1
Tier 1 = 1 triangle
Tier 2 = 5 triangles
Tier 3 = 13 triangles
Tier 4 = 27 triangles
Tier 5 = 48 triangles
Tier 6 = 78 triangles
Tier 7 = 118 triangles
Tier 8 = 170 triangles
Total = 460 triangles

2

Start

ACTIVITY 15

1

2

ACTIVITY 16

1

2

10mm

5mm   5mm

ACTIVITY 17

Self-correcting

ACTIVITY 18

Self-correcting

ACTIVITY 19

1 *Self-correcting*

2 *Self-Correcting*

3 *Self-correcting*

ACTIVITY 20

1 143 × 1 = 143 × 7 = 1001
143 × 2 = 286 × 7 = 2002
143 × 3 = 429 × 7 = 3003 etc

2 864197532. It contains the digits 1 to 9, but not in the correct order

3 *Self-correcting*

General knowledge and vocabulary

ACTIVITY 1

1 scissors, 2 Australia, 3 radish, 4 April, 5 j, 6 flowers, 7 last, 8 insect,
9 fourteen, 10 25th

ACTIVITY 2

1 swarm, 2 snakes, 3 above, 4 racquet 5 hare, 6 apples, 7 tree, 8 Everest,
9 lemon, 10 stethoscope

ACTIVITY 3

1 thermometer, 2 orchard, 3 sergeant, 4 St Patrick, 5 camel, 6 Wellington,
7 eagle, 8 compass, 9 golf, 10 eleven

ACTIVITY 4

1 Tokyo, 2 green, 3 hummingbird, 4 eight, 5 lion, 6 magnet, 7 lodge,
8 diamonds, 9 explorer, 10 1992

ACTIVITY 5

1 astronomer, 2 cheetah, 3 explorer, 4 China, 5 four, 6 police, 7 meat,
8 Northern Territory, 9 elevator, 10 cricketer

ACTIVITY 6

1 fish, 2 meat, 3 cereals, 4 dogs, 5 oceans, 6 scales, 7 year, 8 stable,
9 metals, 10 reptiles

ACTIVITY 7

1 clean, 2 video, 3 vacant, 4 snow, 5 cuff, 6 bouquet, 7 planets, 8 kitchen,
9 detergent, 10 boundary

ACTIVITY 8

1 oasis, 2 rungs, 3 hermit, 4 decade, 5 submarine, 6 turbine, 7 aviary,
8 mutton, 9 purse, 10 cabin

ACTIVITY 9

1 rink, 2 modern, 3 ass, 4 escalator, 5 weak, 6 sandal, 7 crockery, 8 log,
9 herd, 10 vegetables

ACTIVITY 10

1 century, 2 trees, 3 venison 4 horse, 5 dwelling, 6 contract, 7 fawn, 8 den,
9 daisy, 10 caddie

ACTIVITY 11

1 traitor, 2 glutton, 3 truant, 4 optimist, 5 miser, 6 host, 7 hermit, 8 immigrant,
9 coward, 10 mimic

ACTIVITY 12

1 surgeon, **2** compass, **3** fracture, **4** incubator, **5** horse, **6** shepherd, **7** duet,
8 brewery, **9** equator, **10** ford

ACTIVITY 13

1 franc, **2** composer, **3** Holland, **4** London, **5** Edward, **6** China, **7** New York,
8 flower, **9** 52, **10** blood vessels

ACTIVITY 14

1 in your mouth, **2** your feet, **3** in your ear, **4** vitamin C, **5** backbone, **6** to pump
blood around the body, **7** his nose, **8** your foot, **9** your hair – scalp, **10** your
elbow

ACTIVITY 15

1 matron, **2** jockey, **3** teller, **4** dentist, **5** chemist, **6** herbalist, **7** journalist,
8 tourist, **9** detective, **10** architect

ACTIVITY 16

1 Birds of a **feather** flock **together 2** moccasins **3** drover or farmer (a kelpie
is a sheep or cattle dog) **4** United States of America **5** icebergs **6** disease
7 China **8** Western Australia **9** First man on the moon **10** oak

ACTIVITY 17

1 swan, **2** Pluto, **3** port, **4** summerhouse, **5** tree, **6** colour, **7** lyre-bird, **8** India,
9 trumpet, **10** orphan

ACTIVITY 18

1 cavalry, **2** core, **3** vegetarian, **4** aquarium, **5** vase, **6** wallet, **7** pedestrian,
8 bachelor, **9** orphan, **10** poison

ACTIVITY 19

1 Queensland, **2** Kosciusko, **3** poet, **4** tree, **5** Sydney, **6** kangaroo,
7 bushranger, **8** echidna, **9** Tasmania, **10** soldiers

ACTIVITY 20

1 horizon, **2** dawn, **3** fillets, **4** basement or cellar, **5** lava, **6** hymn, **7** turbine,
8 skeleton, **9** assassin, **10** hangar

Teasers and logical puzzles

ACTIVITY 1

1 Drop the 's' **2** The letter 'r' **3** The second **4** The letter 'r' **5** Because there are more of them

ACTIVITY 2

1 The letter 'm' **2** The second day of the week is Monday. Many people write Tuesday **3** None, it is a hole. **4** 11 **5** Neither – twelve nines are one hundred and eight.

ACTIVITY 3

1 1 2 3 4 5 6 7 8 9 10. Get it! 10 to 1 backwards. **2** 'What do the letters Y E S spell?' **3** tooth aches **4** It won't go at all without winding. **5** They all are.

ACTIVITY 4

1 To tie mules to. **2** No coin could be dated BC, they did not know Jesus Christ was coming. **4** The same number, the boat rises with the water.

ACTIVITY 5

1 Let a little air out of the tyres. **2** Hold the torch outside your ear, insects are attracted to light. **3** Place a sheet of paper under the door and push the key out with the ice-cream stick, then pull the paper back under the door, the key should be on the sheet of paper.

ACTIVITY 6

1 It has caught a mouse, **2** Captain Cook, **3** If it dissolves everything known on Earth, it would dissolve the bottles in which it was to be sold. **4** It is the same upside-down or as a mirror image.

ACTIVITY 7

1 You don't bury survivors. **2** Peacocks don't lay eggs, only peahens do. **3** Peanuts grow under the ground.

ACTIVITY 8

1 The glass was on the lawn outside, indicating the window had been broken from inside. **2** Swimming. **3** The hat had been hung on the end of the barrel.

ACTIVITY 9

1 The flat tyre was on the spare wheel in the boot. **2** The eggs are duck eggs. **3** Ross was a police dog.

ACTIVITY 10

1 If the sign was underwater no-one could read it. **2** 3 **3** How could anyone possibly know what the boy had been dreaming.

ACTIVITY 11

1 To cover pigs. **2** 100 **3** They all have, most have more than 28. **4** ONE WORD **5** Only once. After the first time 24 becomes 21. 24 - 3 =21

ACTIVITY 12

1 N T (nine ten) One Two Three Four Five Six Seven Eight Nine Ten. **2** 12 111 **3** Ten cents and five cents. One is not a five cent piece (ten cents), but one is. **4** 65 **5** Forever

ACTIVITY 13

1 1 hour **2** If he had a widow he would already be dead. **3** Grandson **4** a **5** Sunday

ACTIVITY 14

1 It could only happen at the North Pole. **2** 'What! do you think I'll cut your hair for nothing and buy you an ice-cream?' **3** 18 children and 9 cows.

ACTIVITY 15

1 Use a hubcap to reflect the light from the headlights. **2** The car's brakes were faulty. **3** Put some water in the lamp – the oil will float on top of the water and reach the wick.

ACTIVITY 16

1 The person had committed suicide **2** The candidate must be elected

ACTIVITY 17

1 6 **2** The one cent for January, two cents for February system is better than $1.00 per month. Work it out for yourself and see. **3** His widow could not have died before him.

ACTIVITY 18

1 He lifted the signpost and pointed Kerang in the direction he had come from. **2** The answer is 5. He makes one cigarette from every four butts. As he smokes each of his four cigarettes he has a butt left over to make a fifth cigarette. **3** No. It doesn't matter where you live, a ticket only gives you one chance to win. **4** Water polo or polo.

ACTIVITY 19

1 He took out a match and set fire to the paper bag, burning it up. **2** Seven. Four boys and three girls. **3** 10.59 am. **4** Switzerland does not have a navy.

ACTIVITY 20

1 The children are two of triplets or quads. **2** The same as it is today, he hasn't changed it. **3** (i) Are you sure Kay ate her peas? (ii) Don't tease bees. (iii) Too wise you are Too wise you be I see you are Too wise for me. (iv) Oh, I see your are empty.

Classroom TIMESAVERS

CLASSROOM TIMESAVERS UNLIMITED and MORE CLASSROOM TIMESAVERS UNLIMITED bring you just that.

Each book contains over 180 pages of *fully reproducible* forms, diagrams, awards and certificates plus hundreds of simple illustrations covering dozens of themes.

GEOGRAPHY TIMESAVERS is the first in the series to concentrate on a specific area of the curriculum. The dozens of map outlines, graphs and diagrams will prove a highly valuable aid to all teachers.

Join the thousands of Australian teachers who have already discovered TIMESAVERS – invaluable resources, saving hours of preparation time.

Ashton Scholastic